BIBLE

Student Edition • Grade 1

purposeful design
p u b l i c a t i o n s

Colorado Springs, Colorado

Purposeful Design Publications is the publishing division of the Association of Christian Schools International (ACSI) and is committed to the ministry of Christian school education, to enable Christian educators and schools worldwide to effectively prepare students for life. As the publisher of textbooks, trade books, and other educational resources within ACSI, Purposeful Design Publications strives to produce biblically sound materials that reflect Christian scholarship and stewardship and that address the identified needs of Christian schools around the world.

References to books, computer software, and other ancillary resources in this series are not endorsements by ACSI. These materials were selected to provide teachers with additional resources appropriate to the concepts being taught and to promote student understanding and enjoyment.

Unless otherwise identified, all Scripture quotations are taken from the Holy Bible, New King James Version® (NKJV®), © 1982 by Thomas Nelson, Inc. Used by permission. All rights reserved.

Earth, pg 1, NASA

Printed in the United States of America
18 17 16 15 14   4 5 6 7

Elementary Bible, Grade 1
Purposeful Design Elementary Bible Series
ISBN 978-1-58331-254-4 Student edition   Catalog # 10011

Purposeful Design Publications
A Division of ACSI
PO Box 65130 • Colorado Springs, CO 80962-5130
Customer Service: 800/367-0798 • Website: www.acsi.org

Table of Contents

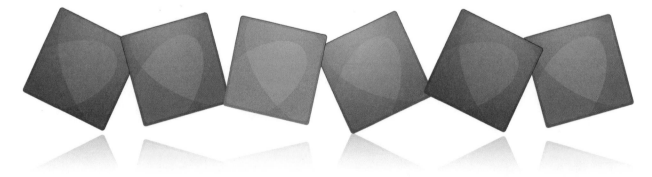

Draw a scene about Creation in the empty circle.

1. Number the days of Creation.

2. On the seventh day, <u>God rested</u>.

1. Make an **X** on the things that were not in the Garden of Eden. Draw two more things that could have been in the Garden.

2. God told Adam and Eve to take care of the earth. Draw a picture of something that you can do to take care of the earth.

Circle the uneaten apple if the picture shows life before the Fall.
Circle the eaten apple if the picture shows life after the Fall.

1.

4.

2.

5.

3.

6.

1. Draw and color a picture of the first family. Put Adam, Eve, Cain, and Abel in your picture.

2. Draw and color a picture of your family.

1. Circle the pictures that show students worshipping God.

God is pleased when you worship Him with a good attitude. Color the heart next to the things that you can do to show your love for God when you worship.

2. praise God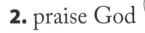

3. chew gum

4. talk to my
neighbor

5. sing

6. read the
Bible

7. pray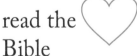

8. sleep

9. listen

10. wiggle

1. Draw a line to match the poor choice on the left to the consequence on the right.

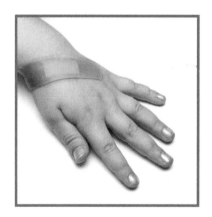

Trace the gray word.

2. God's Word helps me to make good choices.

1. Write the name of the brother who chose to give his best to God.

_____

Cain   Abel

2. Circle the picture of the offering that God accepted.

3. Color the spaces that have a star. Find the hidden word that completes the sentence. Write that word.

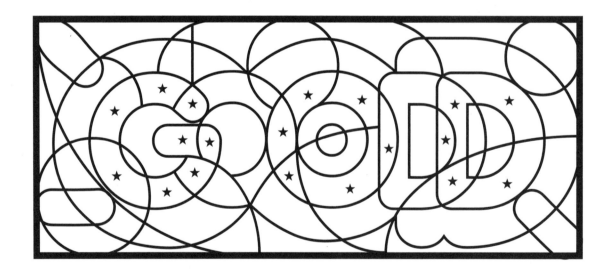

4. When I need help to make wise choices, I will ask _____.

© Bible Grade 1

1. Use the Word Bank to complete the sentences.

God told Noah to build a big _____. The

big boat was the ark. Noah _____ and

obeyed God. Noah worked on the ark for about 100

years! Then the _____ fell. The earth was

flooded. God kept _____ and his family safe.

WORD BANK

boat

Noah

trusted

rain

Color two animals in each row that tell about Noah.

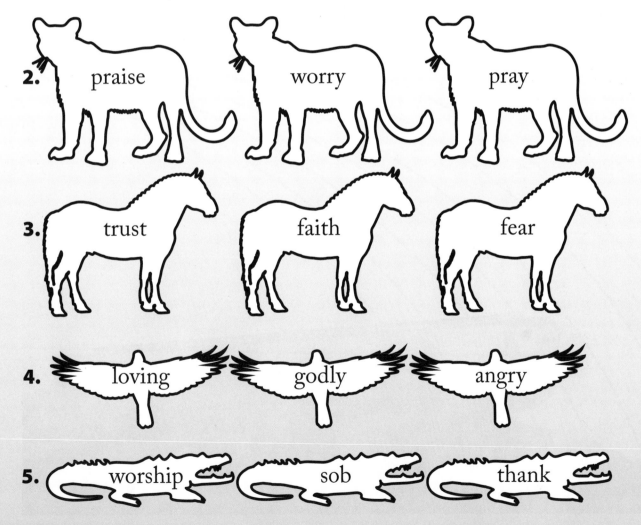

2. praise   worry   pray

3. trust   faith   fear

4. loving   godly   angry

5. worship   sob   thank

Draw a line to match the first part of each sentence to its ending.

1. Noah did what was •   • ark.

2. Noah trusted •   • right.

3. God kept Noah safe in the •   • promise.

4. The rainbow reminds us of God's •   • God.

Color the rainbow.

Listen to each story. Write **yes** or **no** to answer each question.

1. Amina did not like to paint pictures. She did not think that her pictures were as pretty as the other children's pictures. One day her teacher asked her to paint a picture of a flower. Amina didn't want to paint, so she prayed. "God," she said, "Help me to paint a flower." Then Amina painted a beautiful flower! She told her teacher how God had helped her to paint well.

Did Amina bring glory to God? _____

2. Keon liked to help his dad. On Saturday, Keon's dad asked Keon to help rake the leaves and put the leaves in trash bags. Keon thought that the leaves would be too heavy. Keon prayed, "Dear God, help me to lift the heavy bags of leaves to please You and to help my dad." God helped Keon! Keon lifted all the heavy bags. He told his dad how God had helped him.

Did Keon bring glory to God?

_____

1. Circle the pictures of things that Sveta showed her class.

Nesting Dolls

Buildings in Moscow

Samovar

Balalaika

Blini

Иисус любит меня!
Jesus Loves Me!

Trace the gray words.

2. We love others because God loves us.

Abraham moved to the land that God showed him. Think about how Abraham moved.

Write **yes** or **no** to answer each question.

1. Did Abraham have a map? _____

2. Did Abraham have a GPS system? _____

3. Did Abraham have a  moving van? _____

4. Did Abraham stay in a motel room? _____

Do you know what Abraham did have? To find out, unscramble the words below the lines and write them in the correct order.

5. Abraham had _____ _____ _____!

God   in   faith

Read the story.

God kept his promise to . They had a the next year and

named him **Isaac**.

When was older, God told to go to the mountain and

offer as a sacrifice. thought, "I do not understand why

God would ask me to do this, but I trust Him." cut some

wood and loaded it on his . Then , two servants,

and all went to the place of the sacrifice. When they arrived,

 told the servants to stay with the while he and his son

went to worship God.

 had carry the wood. "We have the wood for the fire,

but where is the for the sacrifice, Father?" asked.

looked at and replied, "I am sure that God Himself will provide

the for the offering, my son."

14

Abraham trusted and obeyed God. When you trust and obey your parents, you are learning to trust and obey God.

Listen to each story. Circle the correct picture.

1. Dad told Lindsay to share the laptop computer with her sister Katie, but Lindsay did not want to share. Which picture shows Lindsay obeying Dad?

2. Julie and her brother Ian were having a picture taken. Julie thought that being silly would make the picture look good, but Mom said that smiling faces would make the picture look good. Which picture shows Julie obeying Mom?

Complete the sentence.

3. When I trust and obey my parents, I am learning to trust and

obey _____ .

Think about the story of Mark and Lucas. Listen to each sentence. Fill in the circle in front of the right ending.

1. Mark and his friends loved to _____.

   ○ skateboard   ○ climb trees   ○ ride bikes

2. Mark heard about the fire at Lucas' house, so he and Mom _____.

   ○ went to the park   ○ prayed   ○ played with puzzles

3. Mark felt that God wanted him to _____.

   ○ ignore Lucas   ○ tease Lucas   ○ loan his bike to Lucas

4. When Mark acted on his decision, he made a _____.

   ○ sacrifice   ○ cake   ○ park

5. Part of God's plan for my life is for me to _____.

   ○ ride my bike   ○ serve others   ○ play with toys

Even though Jacob and Esau were twins, they were very different from each other!

Write **J** in the circle if the picture shows something about Jacob. Write **E** in the circle if the picture shows something about Esau.

1.

2.

3.

4.

5.

6.

Use words from the Word Bank to complete the sentences.

WORD BANK

Jacob	father	birthright	blessing
stew	Esau	bread	

1. J_____ tricked his brother, Esau.

2. Esau sold his b_____ for a bowl

of S_____ and some b_____.

3. When he sold his birthright, Esau did not honor his

f_____, Isaac.

4. Jacob lied to his father to get his father's b_____.

5. E_____ planned to kill Jacob!

Listen to the beginning of each sentence and the choices to end each sentence. Put a ✓ by the correct ending.

1. Jacob left his home because

_____ he was going on a fun trip.

_____ he was running away.

_____ he was having a race.

2. Jacob used a stone

_____ for a chair.

_____ to build a house.

_____ for a pillow and an altar.

3. The ladder in Jacob's dream

_____ went from Earth to heaven.

_____ was beside a tree.

_____ was held up by angels.

4. In the unusual dream, God told Jacob,

_____ "Do not sin."

_____ "I am with you."

_____ "Go back home."

Solve the math problems. Match your answer to the letter in the Code Box. Write the letter in the box of the same color at the bottom of the page to discover the new name that God gave to Jacob.

Code Box

1 = P
2 = R
3 = A
4 = D
5 = E
6 = S
7 = L
8 = I

5 + 3 = _____

2 + 4 = _____

1 + 1 = _____

2 + 1 = _____

3 + 2 = _____

4 + 3 = _____

© Bible Grade 1

Use the words below the pictures to complete the sentences.

sun   **stars**   **coins**   **coat**   **moon**   **wheat**

Jacob gave his favorite son, Joseph, a colorful _____.

One night Joseph had a dream that he and his brothers had bundles

of _____. Each of the brothers' bundles bowed

down to Joseph's bundle. Then Joseph had another dream. He

dreamed the _____, _____, and

_____ all bowed down to him. This dream made

his brothers very jealous and angry. They threw Joseph into a pit! They

sold Joseph for 20 silver _____. Joseph was taken

to Egypt as a slave.

Write **yes** on the line if the sentence is true. Write **no** if it is not true.

1. _____ Jacob gave Joseph a beautiful, colorful, long-sleeved coat.

2. _____ Joseph's brothers loved him very much, all the time.

3. _____ Joseph was sold as a slave and was taken to Egypt.

4. _____ Potiphar's wife told the truth about Joseph.

5. _____ Joseph met the pharaoh's son and grandson in prison.

6. _____ Joseph explained the meaning of two prisoners' dreams.

7. Draw a picture of Joseph in prison.

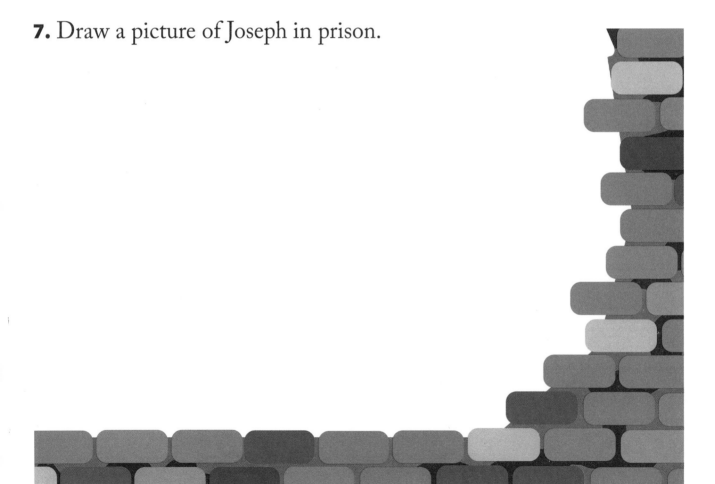

Find out how Joseph saved Egypt. Fill in each blank with the first letter of the picture shown on the pyramid.

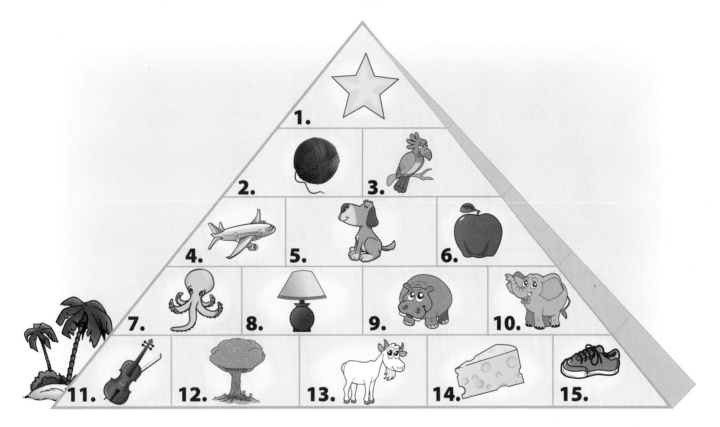

___ ___ ___
13   7   5

___ ___ ___ ___ ___ ___
9   10   8   3   10   5

___ ___ ___ ___ ___ ___
4   7   1   10   3   9

___ ___ ___ ___
1   6   11   10

___ ___ ___ ___ ___.
10   13   2   3   12

1. Megan is sad. Her sister Beth was mean to her. Should Megan forgive Beth? Tell what Megan should do.

2. Matt pushed James on the playground, and James cut his knee. James is hurt, and he is mad at Matt. Should James forgive Matt? Tell what James should do.

3. Luke's brother left some of their toys on the floor. Dad thinks that Luke left the toys out. Now Luke has to pick up the toys. Luke is mad at his brother. Should Luke forgive his brother? Tell what Luke should do.

Use the words on the basket to complete the sentences.

1. The Hebrews had to work

hard as _____.

basket slaves baby

2. Then Pharaoh said to kill all

the _____ boys.

3. Jochebed put her baby in a _____.

Use the words on the pyramid to complete the sentences.

4. Miriam was a brave _____.

5. She watched over _____.

6. Miriam _____ to
Pharaoh's daughter.

saved
girl
Moses
talked

7. God _____
baby Moses.

God told Moses His name. God said, "My name is I AM." God's name is a reminder that God has always been and will always be.

1. Color the sheep that have the letters in God's name, I AM.

Unscramble the words below the lines. Write the words in the correct order.

2. _____ called Moses to

    AM I

_____.

      to   Pharaoh   go

Read each sentence. Draw a line from the sentence to the correct picture.

1. God saved baby Moses.

2. God spoke to Moses from the flames within a burning bush. Moses was willing to serve God.

3. Moses and Aaron went to the palace.

4. God sent frogs up out of the water.

5. God sent hungry grasshoppers.

6. Pharaoh did not let the people go.

Listen to the short stories. Think about how each boy or girl is feeling. What should the children do? Talk about your ideas in your group.

1. Caleb is taking piano lessons. He has to practice for 20 minutes each day. Caleb cannot always find the right notes. He wants to play the piano well. What should Caleb do?

2. Miko doesn't like to eat vegetables, but her mom says that they will make her grow strong. Miko wants to please her mom. What should Miko do?

3. Ivan finds it hard to read and write. Homework is difficult for him, but he wants to do well in school. What should Ivan do?

Read each sentence. Unscramble the letters below each line. Write the word to complete the sentence.

jar   manna   desert   water   quail

1. Moses led the children of Israel across the Red Sea. Then the

people were out in the _____.
                          e e s r d t

2. The people were thirsty. God gave them _____.
                                               t e w a r

3. The people were hungry. The first food that God gave them was

_____.

     n n m a a

4. Then the children of Israel wanted meat. Moses prayed, and God

gave them _____.
          i l q u a

5. To help the people remember God's care, Moses kept some of the

manna in a _____.

          r a j

Listen to each story. Decide which commandment was broken by a poor choice. Write the number on the line provided.

1. Carly's parents would not let her go to her friend's house. Carly went to her room, slammed the door, and pouted. She thought her parents were being unfair!

_____

2. Ken heard older boys in the neighborhood using God's name to curse, so Ken started to talk just like them.

_____

3. Lauren and her sisters played sports each weekend. This left little time for chores, errands, and family time. Her parents chose to not go to church because the family was so busy.

_____

4. Alex liked money so much that nothing was more important to him than getting rich. Money was all Alex could think about.

_____

1
You shall have no other gods before Me.

2
You shall not make for yourself a carved image.

3
You shall not take the name of the Lord your God in vain.

4
Remember the Sabbath day, to keep it holy.

5
Honor your father and your mother.

Listen to each story. Decide which commandment was broken by a poor choice. Write the number.

6 You shall not murder.

7 You shall not commit adultery.

8 You shall not steal.

9 You shall not bear false witness against your neighbor.

10 You shall not covet.

1. Thomas got a brand-new baseball glove for his birthday. Brian did not have a new glove. He was mad and jealous. Brian wanted Thomas' new glove.

_____

2. Jennifer's friend Kelsey started being nice to the new girl in their class. Jennifer was afraid that Kelsey would stop being her friend. Jennifer lied about the new girl to keep Kelsey from playing with the new girl.

_____

3. Ron saw a sparkly, green pencil under Miguel's desk. Ron knew it was Miguel's pencil, but Miguel didn't know it was on the floor. After school, Ron picked up the pencil and took it home.

_____

4. Chelsea borrowed her sister's jacket. Chelsea never gave the jacket back to her sister.

_____

Draw a line to match the words on the left with their descriptions on the right.

Moses •

golden calf •

Mount Sinai •

Ten Commandments •

repent •

consequence •

• the place where God wrote on the stone tablets

• what happens after a choice is made

• the leader of the children of Israel

• a false god; an idol

• the rules that God gave to help guide His people

• to turn away from sin

Joshua and Caleb trusted and obeyed God.
Look for the hidden letters. Write the letters. Read the words.

1. _____ _____ _____ _____ _____

2. _____ _____ _____ _____

3. _____ _____ _____ _____

4. ____ ____ ____ ____ ____ ____ ____ ____

How can you trust and obey God? Use the words to complete
the sentence.

5. I can love the Lord my God with all my _____,

_____, _____, and _____.

Use the words in the Word Bank to complete the sentences.

WORD BANK

Jordan	priests	stones
water	obey	

The Lord told Joshua that it was time to cross the

_____ River into the
Promised Land. Crossing the river seemed impossible,

but Joshua chose to _____
God. Joshua told the people, "When you see the

_____ carrying the ark
of the covenant move, you are to follow them." The
people obeyed! As soon as the priests stepped into the

Jordan River, the _____
stopped flowing, and the people crossed on dry land!
Joshua ordered that the children of Israel make a pile

of 12 _____ to remind
their children of what God had done.

Name _____

Look at the words on the bricks and the descriptions below. Choose the best word or words to fit each description. Write the underlined word.

1. _____
afraid
defeated

2. _____
all-powerful
almighty

3. _____
helpful
saved

4. _____
trusting
obedient

© *Bible* Grade 1

35

Think about what Jimar can do to help Reid learn about God. Draw a line from each sentence to the correct picture.

Bible

kindness

church

1. Jimar can pray for Reid.

2. Jimar can tell Reid about Jesus' death and resurrection.

3. Jimar can give Reid a Bible to read.

4. Jimar can invite Reid to a children's Bible class.

5. Jimar can invite Reid to sit with him in church.

6. Jimar can be kind to Reid even if Reid is not kind to him.

Jesus' death

prayer

Bible class

© *Bible* Grade 1

Gideon was afraid when God chose him to fight the Midianites. Gideon told God that he was not the right man for the job.

Use the code in the box to learn what the angel of the Lord told Gideon and what God wants you to know today.

1. The Lord answered, "_____   _____ _____ _____ _____

_____ _____   _____ _____ _____ _____

_____ _____ _____."

2. When I am afraid, I will remember that _____ _____ _____

_____ _____   _____ _____ _____ _____

_____ _____.

God chose Gideon to lead an army against the Midianites. God helped Gideon to choose the right men to fight against the enemy.

Write **yes** if the sentence tells something true. Write **no** if it does not.

1. Gideon took 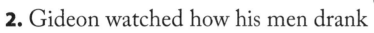 **4,000** men into battle. _____

2. Gideon watched how his men drank  . _____

3. Each of Gideon's men carried a  . _____

4. Each of Gideon's men carried a  . _____

5. Each of Gideon's men blew a  . _____

6. Each of Gideon's men used his ⟼ to destroy

the Midianites. _____

7. God gave Gideon's  the victory. _____

Talk about each picture and discuss how each first grader shows leadership that honors God.

1. Marisol is a cheerleader. She made up two cheers about Jesus and taught them to her friends. Now they cheer for the Lord!

2. DeVon says his Memory Verse to his aunt and uncle. He tells them about the Bible and encourages them to follow God.

3. Greg worships the Lord with his whole heart. He hopes that his brother will follow his example and worship the Lord in the same way.

The Gideons International gives away millions of Bibles and New Testaments every year. These Bibles have helped many, many people come to know the Lord.

Look at the books of the Bible below. Write the correct number to make each sentence true.

1. The Bible is divided into _____ main parts.

2. There are _____ books in the Old Testament.

3. There are _____ books in the New Testament.

4. The Bible contains _____ books in all.

5. God wants to be number _____ in your life!

Old Testament

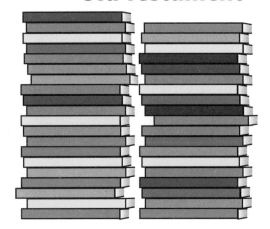

New Testament

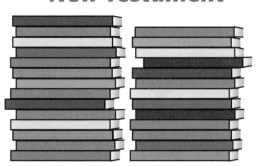

© *Bible Grade 1*

Ruth loved Naomi very much. Ruth was loyal to Naomi. Use the picture word as a clue to complete each promise that Ruth made to Naomi.

family   live   God   stay

1. I will _____ where you _____.

2. I will _____ where you _____.

3. Your _____ will be my _____.

4. Your _____ will be my _____.

Read each riddle. Draw a line to match each riddle with its answer.

Orpah

Ruth

Naomi

Jesus

Boaz

1. I lived in Moab with my husband, sons, and my sons' wives. When the men died, I wanted to move back home. Who am I?

2. I did not go to Bethlehem with Naomi. Who am I?

3. I left with Naomi to take care of her and to worship the one, true God. Who am I?

4. I followed God's laws and became Ruth's kinsman-redeemer. Who am I?

5. I am God's Son. I redeemed all of the people in the world. Who am I?

Look at each picture. Tell something that you would do to help.

1.

3.

2.

4.

5. Choose a picture to write about. List its number here: _____ Write about how you would help the person or people in the picture.

_____

_____

_____

_____

1. Number the pictures in the order that they happened.

2. All of the people pictured pleased God. Share with your classmates some ways that you have chosen to please God.

© Bible Grade 1

Name _____

There are 150 psalms in the book of Psalms. Psalms often tell the feelings of God's people.

Use words from the Word Bank to correctly fill in the blanks. The first letter of each word is gray for you to trace.

WORD BANK

worship	poems	music
Bible	prayers	

1. The book of Psalms is in the middle of the B _____ _____ _____ _____.

2. Some psalms are p _____ _____ _____ _____ _____.

3. Some psalms have been set to m _____ _____ _____ _____.

4. Some psalms are songs for W _____ _____ _____ _____ _____ _____.

5. All of the psalms are p _____ _____ _____ _____.

1. Number the sentences in order to tell about David's life.

_____ David became the king of Israel.

_____ David ran away from King Saul.

_____ David was a shepherd boy.

_____ David played his harp for King Saul.

_____ David killed the giant, Goliath.

_____ David hid from King Saul for many years.

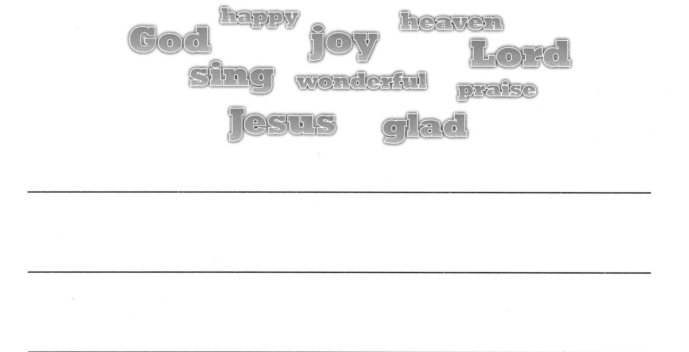

2. Write two sentences of praise. Use some or all of the words below in your sentences.

God   happy   joy   heaven   Lord
sing   wonderful   praise
Jesus   glad

_____

_____

_____

Psalm 23 tells about a good shepherd. Think about the psalm. Write the letter of the picture by the correct sentence.

A. B. C. D.

The Lord is my shepherd. I shall not want.

1. _____ He makes me to lie down in green pastures.

2. _____ He leads me beside the still waters. He restores my soul. He leads me in the paths of righteousness for His name's sake.

3. _____ Yea, though I walk through the valley of the shadow of death, I will fear no evil for You are with me.

4. _____ Your rod and Your staff, they comfort me.

5. How is Jesus like a good shepherd?

_____

_____

Listen to each prayer. Fill in the circle that best describes each prayer.

1. I am sorry for hitting my brother.

○ confession and repentance
○ praise
○ request

2. You are so wonderful, God!

○ confession and repentance
○ praise
○ request

3. Please help my grandmother get over her cold.

○ confession and repentance
○ praise
○ request

4. Teach me to know Your Word better.

○ confession and repentance
○ praise
○ request

5. Copying Cassie's work was wrong. Forgive me, Lord.

○ confession and repentance
○ praise
○ request

© *Bible* Grade 1

Use the words in the Word Bank to complete the sentences.

WORD BANK
| temple | thank | people | God | Solomon |

1. King David had a son named _____.

2. Solomon built the _____.

3. The glory of _____ filled the temple.

4. The _____ worshipped God in the temple.

5. God is pleased when I _____ and praise Him.

Use the Word Bank to help unscramble the words. Write the words correctly to complete the sentences.

WORD BANK		
worship	thank	praise

1. k n t h a   I _____ God for my parents.

2. s e p r a i   I _____ God for His love.

3. r o w p i s h   I _____ God when I bow my head in prayer.

Use the codes below to learn a reason to praise God. Write the reason on the lines.

4. _____ _____ _____ _____.

GOD LOVES YOU!

PSALM 100

Circle the correct word. Write it on the line.

1. Make a _____ noise to the Lord.

sad   glad

2. Come before God and _____.

bird   sing

3. Enter His gates with _____.

thanks   books

4. Enter His courts with _____.

hills   praise

5. The Lord is good. His love lasts _____.

forever   a day

Complete the letter to God. Use your own words.

Oh, give thanks to the Lord!
Call upon His name;
Make known His deeds
among the peoples!
(1 Chronicles 16:8)

Dear _____,

    Thank You for _____

_____ .

I praise You for _____

_____

_____ .

       Love,

       _____

Draw a line to match the first part of each sentence to its ending.

1. King Ahab would not •   • to speak to a widow.

2. Elijah trusted God, and •   • to feed Elijah.

3. God sent ravens •   • stop worshipping Baal.

4. Then God sent Elijah •   • God provided for his needs.

5. The widow trusted God and baked •   • to run out.

6. God did not allow the flour or the oil •   • some bread.

Unscramble the letters to complete the sentences.

1. Elijah had no water and no ____ ____ ____ ____. (o f o d)

2. The widow only had a little ____ ____ ____ ____ ____. (o r u f l)

3. The widow had only a small jar of ____ ____ ____. (i o l)

4. Both Elijah and the widow had faith in ____ ____ ____. (G d o)

Write the letters from the green spaces on the lines below.

5.

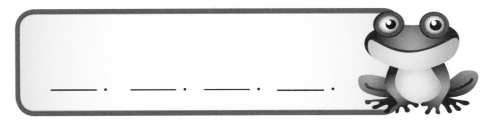

____ . ____ . ____ . ____ .

6. These initials stand for **f**ully **r**elying **o**n **G**od. Elijah and the widow relied on God. Tell how God provided for their needs. Color the picture.

_____

_____

_____

Name _____

God showed His power and love for Elijah and the widow through His miracles.

Use words from the Word Bank to complete the sentences.

The widow showed hospitality to Elijah, and the Lord provided for her needs. Her flour and oil did not run out. She baked bread for Elijah and gave him a room in her home.

WORD BANK

alive
truth
sick
prayed
died
miracle

One day, the widow's son got _____. He

was so sick that he _____. The widow

was very, very sad! She spoke to Elijah. Elijah took the boy to his own

room and _____ to the Lord. The Lord

answered Elijah's prayer with a _____.

The boy was _____ again! Now the

widow knew that Elijah spoke the _____.

Circle the better answer. Underline words that show hospitality.

1. Beth's friend moved away. Beth still feels sad. Now a new girl is moving into the house where Beth's friend had lived. How can Beth show hospitality?

○ make a picture to welcome the new family

○ feel sad and do nothing

2. Victor likes to play soccer with his friends, but he does not want his new soccer ball to get dirty. How can Victor show hospitality?

○ keep his soccer ball at home

○ share his soccer ball with his friends

3. Ting's teacher asked her to help a new student, but Ting is shy. How can Ting show hospitality?

○ be friendly and talk to the new student

○ ask her teacher to get someone else to help the new student

4. Nathan's grandmother needs a soft bed when she comes to visit. Nathan has a soft bed. How can Nathan show hospitality?

○ be grumpy about giving up his bed

○ be happy to let his grandmother use his bed

Elijah held a contest to show the king and the people that the Lord God was the only true God. Read each statement.

Circle God's altar if the statement is true.

Circle Baal's altar if the statement is not true.

1. King Ahab would not stop worshipping Baal.

2. Two altars were set up on Mount Carmel.

3. There were 500 false prophets of Baal.

4. Baal could hear the prayers of the false prophets.

5. Elijah had water poured over God's altar.

6. Elijah prayed, and God sent fire from heaven.

7. The people turned back to the Lord.

Elijah gathered the Israelites on Mount Carmel to prove that the Lord was the real God.

1. Number the sentences to show how Elijah prepared the altar.

_____ Elijah piled wood on top of the stones.

_____ Elijah had an altar built with 12 large stones.

_____ Elijah had a sacrifice put on the wood.

2. Number the sentences to show what Elijah did next.

_____ Elijah had water poured over the altar three times.

_____ Elijah dug a ditch around the altar.

_____ Elijah had four waterpots filled with water.

3. Number the sentences to show what happened when God showed His power.

_____ Fire came from heaven.

_____ The people turned back to God.

_____ The fire burned up the sacrifice, the wood, the stones, the water, and even the dirt!

False prophets do not tell the truth. The Bible tells the truth.

The sentences near the bottom of the page are not true. Write the letter of the Bible verse that corrects each untrue sentence.

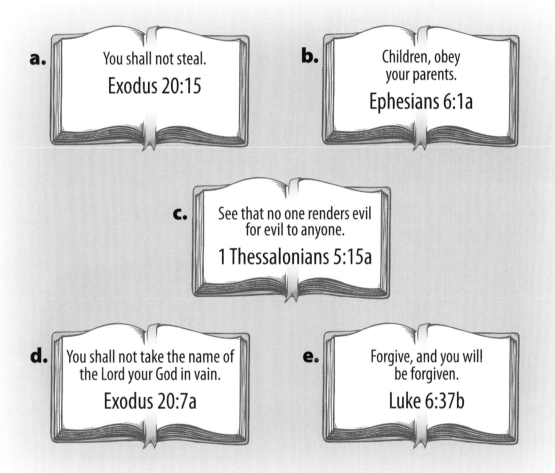

a. You shall not steal.
Exodus 20:15

b. Children, obey your parents.
Ephesians 6:1a

c. See that no one renders evil for evil to anyone.
1 Thessalonians 5:15a

d. You shall not take the name of the Lord your God in vain.
Exodus 20:7a

e. Forgive, and you will be forgiven.
Luke 6:37b

1. Using God's name to curse is no big deal. Everybody does it. _____

2. It is okay to take a toy from the store without paying for it. _____

3. You do not have to forgive people who hurt you. _____

4. It is not important to obey your parents. _____

5. If someone is mean to you, you should be mean in return! _____

1. Yoon sees his friends in the park. Yoon wants to share the good news about Jesus with his friends. Circle some ways that Yoon can share his faith.

Yoon can pray for his friends.

Yoon can invite his friends to go to church.

Yoon can be kind to his friends and explain that God loves them.

2. Traci wants her best friend, Autumn, to know about Jesus. Circle some ways that Traci can share her faith with Autumn.

Traci can pray for Autumn.

Traci can give Autumn a book of Bible truths for children.

Traci can tell Autumn about what she has learned in Bible class.

3. Taye wants his neighbor, Hudson, to learn about Jesus. Circle some ways that Taye can share his faith with his neighbor.

Taye can explain that Jesus died on the cross for everyone.

Taye can invite Hudson to go to church with him.

Taye can pray for Hudson.

King Josiah learned to make wise choices when he was young.

Read each sentence. Think about the choice that was made. Was it a wise choice or a foolish choice? Some sentences are true, but they tell of foolish choices. Underline the letter after each wise choice.

1. King Josiah learned God's Word. **B**

2. King Josiah followed King David's example. **I**

3. Many people worshipped idols. **T**

4. King Josiah got rid of all the idols. **B**

5. The people did not take care of the temple. **R**

6. King Josiah gave money to fix the temple. **L**

7. The people forgot God's laws. **K**

8. King Josiah read God's laws and obeyed them. **E**

Use the letter that is beside each wise choice to make the word that completes the sentence.

9. I can make wise choices by studying the

_____ and doing what it says.

It is important for you to begin the habit of reading the Bible when you are young, just as King Josiah did.

Look at each picture and listen to the sentences below. Write the number of the sentence in the corner of the matching picture.

1. Alaina's mom reads the Bible to Alaina every night when Alaina is in bed.

2. Every day, Niki reads some words in the Bible by herself.

3. Annie's dad reads the Bible each evening at dinnertime.

4. Celina's mom and dad read the Bible to Celina and her younger brother at bedtime.

5. Armando's mom and dad read the Bible and pray together.

6. What is your favorite time to read the Bible?

_____

_____

You can discover many wonderful things in God's Word if you look!

To find a hidden picture in the box below, listen to each Bible verse and the sentence. When you hear the missing word, color the space in the box with that word.

1. Psalm 50:15: I can _____ on the Lord to help me, and He will!

2. Psalm 32:8: The Lord will _____ me and watch over me.

3. Proverbs 29:25: The Lord will keep me _____.

4. 1 John 1:9: The Lord will _____ my sins.

5. 1 John 5:14–15: The Lord _____ my prayers.

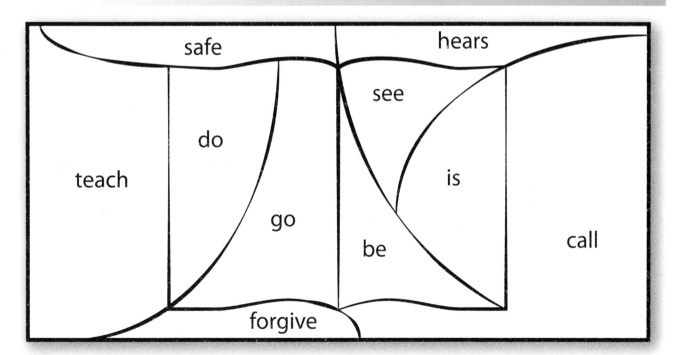

Complete the sentence.
6. I discover God's promises when I read God's _____.

1. Circle the pictures of the things that Emma and her mother learned about China by reading a book.

THE GREAT WALL

CHINESE WRITING

PANDAS

HIGH MOUNTAINS

FIREWORKS

PAPER LANTERNS

2. Emma has begun to help her new friend, Ming, to learn English. Tell how Emma can share God's Word with Ming.

_____

_____

_____

© Bible Grade 1

Use the words at the bottom of the page to complete the sentences.

Joseph and Mary took a long trip to Bethlehem to be

counted. When they reached Bethlehem, they had to

stay in a _____ because there was no room in

the inn. That very night, the baby Jesus was born! Mary wrapped Him

in soft cloths and laid Him in a _____.

Out in the fields, some shepherds were watching their sheep. An

_____ told them that the Savior had been

born! The angel told them to go to Bethlehem. They left their

_____ and went to Bethlehem. They found

the baby and praised God!

manger   sheep   stable   angel

1. Color the boxes that tell about Joseph and Mary presenting Jesus to God in the temple.

Joseph and Mary brought baby Jesus to the temple.

Some shepherds went with them to the temple.

Simeon took the baby in his arms and praised God.

Simeon told Joseph and Mary that Jesus had been born to save all people from their sins.

Anna joyfully told many people that the Messiah had come.

Read each story. Discuss the answers in class.

2. Ramón is tired of waiting to open his Christmas gifts. How can Ramón be like Simeon and wait patiently with a good attitude?

3. Pierre and Philippe celebrate Christmas in their home in Haiti. How can they be like Anna and share the good news of the Savior?

Angels are God's messengers. Draw a line from each angel's message on the left to the person or people who received the message.

1. You will find the baby wrapped in cloths and lying in a manger. •

• Mary

2. You will be the mother of the promised Savior.
•

• shepherds

3. Move your family to Egypt. •

• Joseph

Find the words that correctly complete each sentence. Connect the dots in the order of the sentences. Color the picture.

4. The wise men followed a _____.

5. The wise men brought _____.

6. The wise men worshipped _____.

7. The wise men were warned in a _____.

8. The wise men did not return to _____.

star

Jesus

dream

King Herod

gifts

1. What gifts have you received from Jesus? Circle the words that tell about His gifts to you.

eternal life   joy

peace   hope

His Word   prayer

forgiveness   love

2. What can you give back to the Lord? Circle the words that tell about gifts you can give to Him.

praise

worship

a good attitude

a heart filled with joy

gifts for others with needs

© *Bible Grade 1*

Joseph trusted God when he obeyed God's direction to take Jesus and Mary to Egypt.

How can you show others that you trust in God? Put each group of words in order to make a sentence. Write the sentence.

1. I   kind.   can   be

_____

2. I   tell   can   truth.   the

_____

3. I   read   can   Bible.   my

_____

4. I   pray   for   can   others.

_____

1. How old was Jesus when He went to Jerusalem? Choose the number that tells Jesus' age. Look in the puzzle for that number. Each time you see that number, circle the letter below it. Then, write the correct letters in order on the blank lines below.

10	8	11	6	12	4	9	12	7	10
X	N	A	O	T	R	S	E	W	Y

5	12	9	8	10	12	4	11	7	13
U	M	Z	I	K	P	B	J	C	E

6	8	10	12	11	9	7	5	4	12
D	S	A	L	R	N	O	T	V	E

Joseph and Mary found Jesus in the ____ ____ ____ ____ ____ ____.

2. Draw a picture of Jesus talking to the religious teachers in the temple.

Jesus made wise choices, and you can too! Decide if each sentence shows a wise or unwise choice. Check the correct box.

	Wise	*Unwise*
1. Listen to your teachers.		
2. Talk during someone's prayer.		
3. Obey your parents.		
4. Push your friend.		
5. Tell a lie.		
6. Go to church.		
7. Study God's Word.		

Fill in the circle in front of the wise choice.

1. At the park, a little boy tried to take Simon's ball. What should Simon do?

○ He should push the boy and tell him not to take the ball.

○ He should ask the boy to join him in a game.

○ He should get mad and go home.

2. LaShondra is not supposed to use her mom's phone, but she wants to play with it. What should LaShondra do?

○ She should make a phone call.

○ She should leave her mom's phone alone.

○ She should play a game on the phone.

3. David and Kami watched TV, but the show started to use bad language. What should they do?

○ They should turn off the television and play a game.

○ They should watch the show until it is over.

○ They should watch the show but say "beep" at the bad words.

Draw a line that connects the beginning of each sentence to its correct ending.

1. Jesus went to the •   • book of Isaiah.

2. He stood up •   • synagogue to worship.

3. He read from the •   • because it is true.

4. Jesus told the people that He •   • to read.

5. I can believe the Bible •   • was reading about Himself.

Use a blue crayon or marker to color all the shapes that have a dot. Write the hidden word to complete the sentence.

6. God's Word is _____.

Circle and write the correct word or words that complete each sentence.

1. God's Word is called the _____.

cup   Bible   cloud

2. God told _____ what to say in the Bible.

people   dogs   plants

3. The Bible is God's _____.

truth   rock   pet

4. The Bible helps me to _____.

eat lunch   know God   tie shoes

5. God's Word lasts _____.

a minute   a day   forever

Listen to the Bible verses your teacher reads. Follow your teacher's directions.

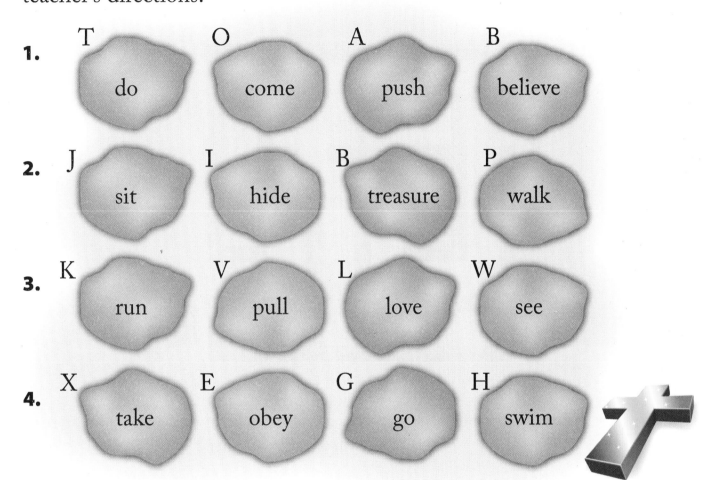

1. T do   O come   A push   B believe

2. J sit   I hide   B treasure   P walk

3. K run   V pull   L love   W see

4. X take   E obey   G go   H swim

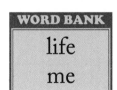

5. The _____ _____ _____ _____ _____ is God's Word.

Use the Word Bank to complete each sentence.

WORD BANK
life
me

6. God's Word guides _____.

7. God's Word promises me eternal _____.

1. God's Word contains many treasures. Find the correct pathway to the treasure box.

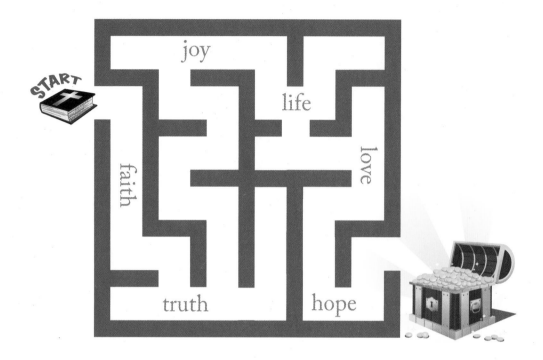

2. Write the words from the maze that name some of God's treasures.

_____   _____   _____

_____   _____   _____

3. Write the words of Psalm 119:11.

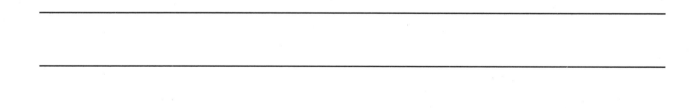

_____

_____

_____

_____

Use the code to find Jesus' words.

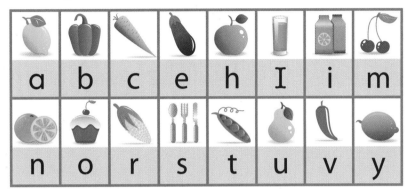

Jesus said, "__ __ __ __ __ __

__ __ __ __, __ __ __ __ __ __

__ __ __ __ __ __ __ __ __ __ __ __."

John 15:5a

Fill in the circle beside the word or words that best complete each sentence.

1. Jesus chose ____ men to be His followers.
- ○ 5
- ○ 12
- ○ 7

2. Jesus' followers were called ____.
- ○ disciples
- ○ desks
- ○ doors

3. The first disciples chosen by Jesus were ____, ____, ____, and ____.
- ○ Matthew, Mark, Luke, John
- ○ Peter, Paul, Andrew, John
- ○ Peter, Andrew, James, John

4. Jesus told them, "From now on, you will catch ____."
- ○ fish
- ○ colds
- ○ people

5. Catching people means ____ people to Jesus.
- ○ asking
- ○ finding
- ○ leading

Jesus told His disciples to obey the Great Commission and tell people everywhere the good news that He has saved them from their sins.

How can you follow the Great Commission? Circle the fish that show ways to obey Jesus' command.

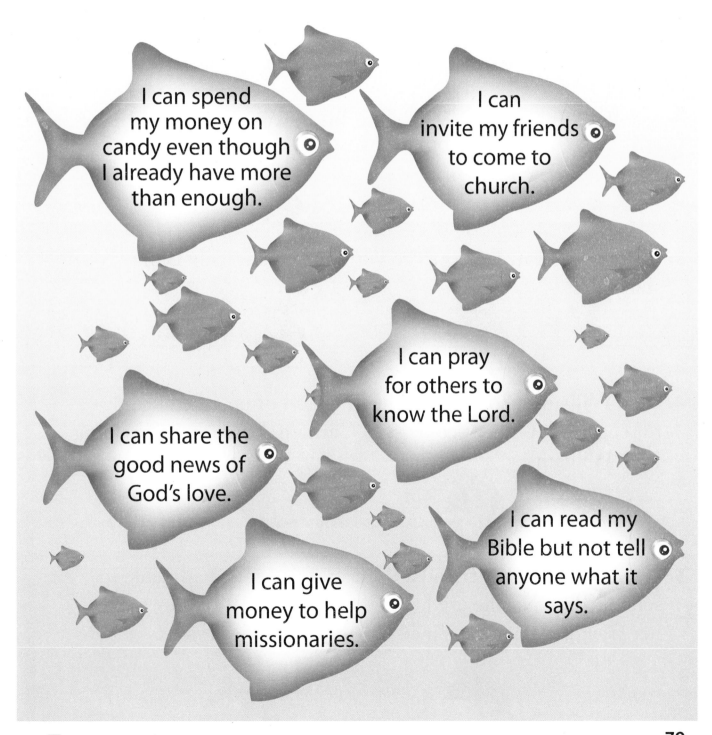

I can spend my money on candy even though I already have more than enough.

I can invite my friends to come to church.

I can pray for others to know the Lord.

I can share the good news of God's love.

I can read my Bible but not tell anyone what it says.

I can give money to help missionaries.

Listen to each story about a first grader. Circle the grapes if the child is showing the fruit of the Spirit. Circle the fish if the child is leading someone to have faith in Jesus.

1. Terrell showed his little brother how to tie his shoes. Terrell had to show his brother many times before his brother could tie the shoes.

2. Livia's team lost the basketball game, but she chose to have a good attitude and not pout about the loss.

3. Santiago invited Tomás to go with him to a weekly Bible study class.

4. Mrs. Williams had difficulty hearing and often asked people to repeat what other people said. Carmen did not mind helping Mrs. Williams.

5. Natalie showed her friend a Bible craft that she had made in school. Then Natalie used the craft to tell the Bible story to her friend. Natalie explained that Jesus loves everyone!

Read the story.

One day and His disciples were walking through Samaria.

 met a at a . He asked the for a drink of

 . The did not understand why would speak so

kindly to her, but she listened to Him. offered the

living . knew all about the woman's sins. The

was amazed that knew all about her. She wanted to be

forgiven and to go to heaven. told the that He was

the Messiah. The was so excited that she left her at

the well. She told many other people in the town that she had

met Jesus, the Messiah.

Fill in the correct circles. There may be more than one answer.

1. Kaylani hit Sean because he called her a bad name. What should they do to make things right again?

- ○ They should tell each other what they did wrong.
- ○ They should say they are sorry for what they did.
- ○ They should ask God and each other for forgiveness.

2. Natani copied Kris' answers to the math test. What should Natani do to make things right again?

- ○ She should tell Kris what she did and ask her for forgiveness.
- ○ She should tell her teacher that she copied the answers.
- ○ She should ask God to forgive her for cheating.

3. Ryan and Mack got into a fight at recess. What should they do to make things right again?

- ○ They should tell each other that they are sorry for fighting.
- ○ They should ask God to forgive them.
- ○ They should ask each other for forgiveness.

Read each exercise. Decide if the actions show Jesus' love. If so, color the heart beside the exercise.

1. Taylor noticed that Luke fell at recess. Taylor helped Luke up and went to get him a bandage.

2. Mary did not want to be in the same reading group as Joel because Joel read slowly. She complained about this to others.

3. Pravaas helped his teacher put the library books on the shelves.

4. Whitney was upset because she lost a game to Lauren. Whitney called Lauren a cheater.

5. Mrs. Cook was on recess duty. The children left all of the playground toys outside when they went in. No one offered to help Mrs. Cook pick up the toys.

6. Think of something you can do to show kindness to someone. Write your idea on the lines.

_____

_____

_____

Jesus showed kindness to the Samaritan woman at the well.

1. Write your name in the middle oval. Write in the outer ovals the names of people to whom you plan to share kindness.

2. Think about someone you would like to talk to about God's plan of salvation. Write his or her name on the line. In class, share what you would say to that person.

_____

A boy shared his lunch with Jesus. Jesus used the boy's food to feed many, many people!

Look at the numbers in the box. Write the number that matches each picture.

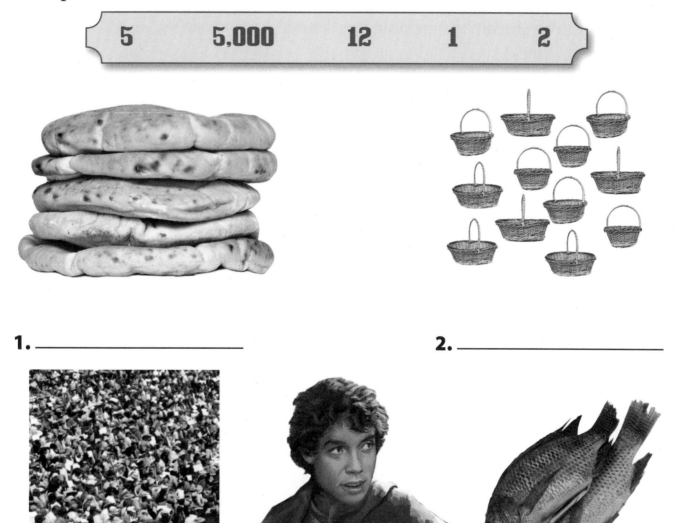

5   5,000   12   1   2

1. _____   **2.** _____

3. _____   **4.** _____   **5.** _____

Use the pictures to help retell today's Bible truth.

Jesus taught His disciples about Himself through His miracles. Fill in the circle next to the correct ending for each sentence. There may be more than one correct ending.

1. Jesus did miracles because

○ He cared about the people.

○ He wanted the people to give glory to God.

○ He wanted something to eat.

2. The disciples learned that God is

○ loving and all-powerful.

○ always hungry.

○ able to be trusted.

3. Jesus taught His disciples to

○ trust in Him.

○ pay for food.

○ use whatever they had in faith.

4. Jesus is pleased when

○ Christians share what they have with others.

○ Christians act selfishly.

○ Christians thank Him for His gifts.

Read each sentence and trace the gray words. These words describe God.

1. God is caring.

2. God is generous and giving.

3. God is all-powerful.

4. God is faithful to keep His promises.

God's miracles show His character traits. Draw a line to match each sentence to the picture it describes. Talk about what each miracle teaches you about God's character.

5. Gideon leads the army of 300.

6. Elijah meets the widow.

7. Jesus feeds 5,000.

8. Elijah prays for fire.

Use the code to solve the puzzle about sharing.

I	i	o	n	G	r	w	s	a	h	e	d	t
20	10	8	24	12	25	15	3	13	22	11	26	2

$\overline{}$ 20 $\qquad$ $\overline{}$ 22 $\overline{}$ 8 $\overline{}$ 24 $\overline{}$ 8 $\overline{}$ 25

$\overline{}$ 12 $\overline{}$ 8 $\overline{}$ 26 $\qquad$ $\overline{}$ 15 $\overline{}$ 22 $\overline{}$ 11 $\overline{}$ 24 $\qquad$ $\overline{}$ 20

$\overline{}$ 3 $\overline{}$ 22 $\overline{}$ 13 $\overline{}$ 25 $\overline{}$ 11 $\qquad$ $\overline{}$ 15 $\overline{}$ 10 $\overline{}$ 2 $\overline{}$ 22

$\overline{}$ 8 $\overline{}$ 2 $\overline{}$ 22 $\overline{}$ 11 $\overline{}$ 25 $\overline{}$ 3 .

© Bible Grade 1

Four friends helped their sick friend. Jesus forgave the man and healed him.

Draw a line to match each person or group of people with the words they said or might have said.

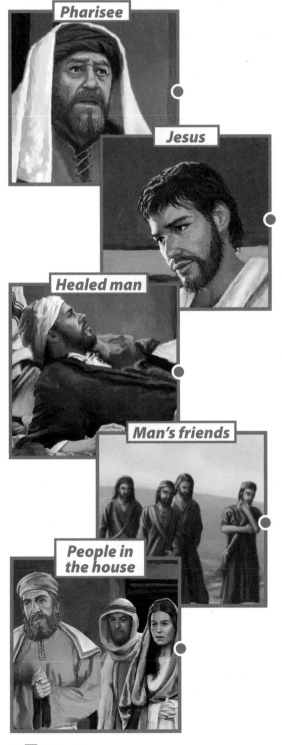

Pharisee

Jesus

Healed man

Man's friends

People in the house

"Thank you for healing me!"

"Only God can forgive sins!"

"Let's be careful. We don't want to hurt our friend."

"What is going on up on the roof?"

"Your sins are forgiven. Pick up your mat and walk."

The paralyzed man's friends did not let anything keep them from taking their friend to Jesus. They had faith in Jesus!

1. Find the correct pathway from the friends to Jesus.

2. Write the words that tell things that could have kept the friends from reaching Jesus.

_____   _____

_____

Choose three things that the orphans in North Korea needed. Write each choice on the line. Draw a picture of the things you chose.

food   clothes   a place to live

medical care   education   knowing about Jesus

Needs	*My Picture*
_____ _____	
_____ _____	
_____ _____	

1. Cross out each of the letters **X**, **Y**, and **Z**. Write the remaining letters to find the answer to the question below.

X	X	H	E	Y	Z	F	O	R	G	A	V
E	Z	T	H	E	X	Z	M	A	N	S	Y
X	S	I	N	S	Y	Y	Z	A	N	D	Y
H	E	A	L	E	D	X	Y	Z	H	I	M

HOW DID JESUS HELP THE PARALYZED MAN?

___ _____ ____

,

_____ __ _____ ___

_____ _____.

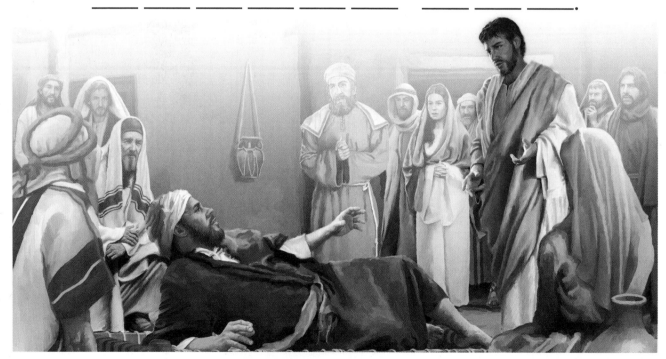

Read the poem. Write a number word to answer each question.

As Jesus walked from Galilee
He met ten men with leprosy.
They called to Him; their cries increased.
So Jesus said, "Go to the priests."
Because of Jesus' love and power,
All ten were healed within the hour.
Nine went happily on their way.
Just one gave thanks to the Lord that day.

1. How many men had leprosy? _____

2. How many men did Jesus heal? _____

3. How many men went on their way and did not return to give

thanks to the Lord? _____

4. How many men returned to thank Jesus? _____

Read the words below the box. Color the words using the color key.

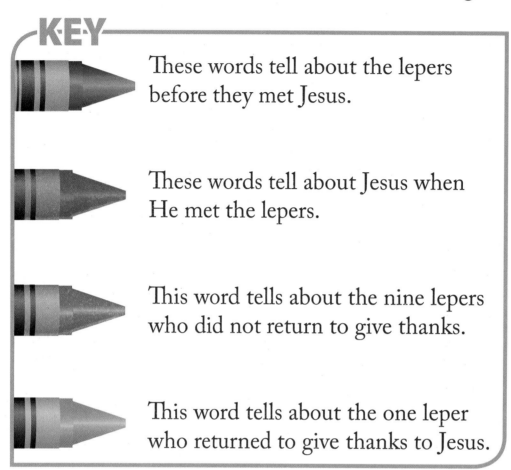

KEY

These words tell about the lepers before they met Jesus.

These words tell about Jesus when He met the lepers.

This word tells about the nine lepers who did not return to give thanks.

This word tells about the one leper who returned to give thanks to Jesus.

sad lonely loving sick thankful unclean powerful ungrateful

Gregory did not appreciate his many blessings. He did not thank the people who provided blessings to him. What about you? Do you always remember to thank others?

1. Put a check mark ✓ in the box next to any of the things that you sometimes forget to be thankful for. Write the name of someone you need to thank next to the things you checked.

☐ good food _____

☐ someone to play with _____

☐ help with homework _____

☐ a ride to school _____

☐ an interesting lesson _____

☐ a clean classroom _____

What things will you try to remember to give thanks for each day?

2. _____ **4.** _____

3. _____ **5.** _____

Listen to each story. Underline the words that show mercy or grace.

1. Anita's little sister always wants to follow Anita around. Anita does not want to play with her sister all day. What should Anita say to her?

"I'll play with you for a little while today."

"Go away and don't bother me anymore!"

2. Cassidy's brother was mad at her, so he called her a bad name. That made Cassidy mad. What should Cassidy say to her brother?

"I'm telling Mom! I hope you get in big trouble."

"I don't like fighting. Let's stop it now."

3. Vanessa took Gavin's place in line. Gavin felt angry about that. What should Gavin say to Vanessa?

"I was here first, but you may have my place in line today."

"Go to the back of the line now! You know that cutting in line is against the rules."

4. Pretend that you are a friend of Anita, Cassidy, or Gavin. Discuss in class what words you could use to show mercy or grace to them.

Read the sentences and the words on the coins. Color the coin that best completes each sentence.

1. Jesus and His disciples were in the _____.

2. Jesus watched people put money into the _____.

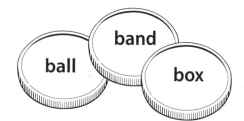

3. Some rich people put in a lot of _____.

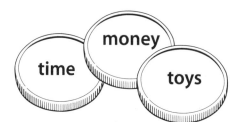

4. One poor widow put in two copper _____.

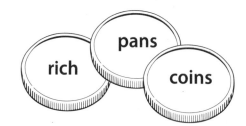

5. Jesus pointed out the widow because she gave away money that she _____.

Each sentence shows faith and trust in God. Match the sentence on the left with the way the person or people trusted on the right.

1. Peter let down his fishing nets. •

2. A boy gave his lunch to Jesus. •

3. Four friends brought their sick friend to Jesus. •

4. Ten lepers begged for healing. •

5. A poor widow put all of her money into a special box in the temple. •

• They trusted Jesus to heal their friend.

• He trusted Jesus to feed the people.

• They trusted Jesus to heal them.

• She trusted God to provide for her needs.

• He trusted Jesus to provide a catch of fish.

Choose the correct word to complete each sentence.

1. The Lord is pleased when I spend my

_____ serving others.

possessions
time
talents

2. I am being a good steward when I share my money and my other

_____ with people in need.

3. When I use my special skills, or _____, to

help tell others about Jesus, I please God.

4. The best reason to be a good steward is to please God. List some
ways you use your time, talents, and possessions to please God.

_____

_____

_____

Read the sentences and look at the pictures. Decide if the child is showing good stewardship or poor stewardship of God's gifts. Fill in the correct circle.

1. Keisha recycles her family's plastic bottles, cans, and cardboard.

    ○ good stewardship   ○ poor stewardship

2. Mindy takes more food than she can eat and ends up throwing some food away.

    ○ good stewardship   ○ poor stewardship

3. Trevor makes paper airplanes instead of drawing pictures during art class.

    ○ good stewardship   ○ poor stewardship

4. Josef put a paper that he did not need in the recycle bin instead of throwing it on the floor.

    ○ good stewardship   ○ poor stewardship

Number each group of sentences in the correct order to retell the Bible truth. Use numbers 1–4 for the first group of sentences. Use numbers 5–9 for the second group of sentences.

_____ The disciples were afraid of the wind and waves.

_____ Jesus sent the disciples across the lake in a boat.

_____ A storm came up on the lake.

_____ Jesus walked on top of the water!

_____ The disciples worshipped Jesus as the Son of God.

_____ Peter stepped out of the boat and began to walk on water.

_____ Peter began to sink, and Jesus saved him.

_____ Peter took his eyes off of Jesus and looked at the storm.

_____ Peter asked to come to Jesus.

Match each clue with a word from the Word Bank. Copy each letter on a shaded line onto the boat to discover what Peter needed to do to keep from sinking.

WORD BANK

fishermen
storm
disciples
Peter
sunk

1. high winds and waves ____ ____ ____ ____ ____

2. what some disciples were before they met Jesus

____ ____ ____ ____ ____ ____ ____ ____ ____

3. had gone down into the water ____ ____ ____ ____

4. Jesus' followers

____ ____ ____ ____ ____ ____ ____ ____ ____

5. the disciple who stepped out of the boat ____ ____ ____ ____ ____

6. ____ ____ ____ ____ ____

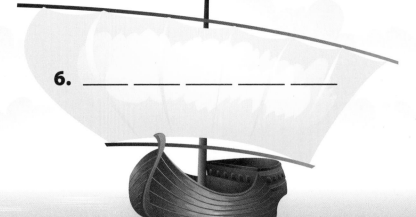

Read each story. Mark the choice that shows trust instead of fear.

1. Ann is good at spelling, but she is very shy. Monday is the big Spelling Bee, and Ann is afraid. What should Ann do?

○ She should misspell a word that she knows so that she can sit down.
○ She should pray and then do her best.
○ She should stay home from school.

2. Ben is afraid to jump into the deep end of the pool, but Dad says he will catch him. What should Ben do?

○ He should stay out of the pool.
○ He should go play with his little brother.
○ He should pray, trust his dad, and jump in!

3. Lexie has a chance to ride in a hot air balloon. Her family wants her to go up with them, but she is afraid. What should Lexie do?

○ She should cry.
○ She should remember how Jesus helped Peter when Peter was afraid and then trust Jesus to help her go up in the balloon.
○ She should stay on the ground.

Listen to what the Bible says about trust. Write the verse reference next to the correct picture.

Psalm 56:3   Psalm 44:6–7   Proverbs 3:5   Proverbs 11:28

1. It is better to trust in God than to give in to fear.

_____

2. It is better to trust in God than to trust in weapons.

_____

3. It is better to trust in God than to trust in money.

_____

4. It is better to trust in God than to trust in your own understanding.

_____

Read the sentences. Write **yes** if the sentence tells something from the Bible truth. Write **no** if it does not.

1.  went to visit Mary, Martha, and Lazarus. _____

2. Martha did not welcome Jesus into her  . _____

3. Mary sat at Jesus'  and listened to His Word. _____

4. Martha was busy making and serving . Martha saw that

Mary was not helping. _____

5. Martha used the  to clean the floor. _____

6. Jesus said that listening to His Word was the most important

thing. Mary had put Jesus **FIRST** . _____

Read the story.

Lazarus, Come Out!

 Mary  Martha  Jesus  Lazarus  tomb

 and were sad. was very sick. and

asked to help. They said, " is sick."

 did not come right away. died and was put in a .

Then came. said, "If you had been here, would not

have died."

 went to the . He said, ", come out!" came out!

 is never too late!

Name _____

Believing God 27.3

Solve each math problem and write the answer underneath. Match the answers with the letters to fill in the sentences. Read the story. Color the picture.

1 + 1	2 + 2	3 + 3	4 + 4	5 + 5	6 + 6	7 + 7	8 + 8	9 + 9	10 + 10
h	v	g	f	o	a	i	l	t	e

Mary had so much ____ ____ ____ ____ for Jesus. She wanted
              16   10   4   20

to honor Jesus with a ____ ____ ____ ____. Judas said Mary had
           6   14   8   18

wasted her perfume! Jesus knew that Mary ____ ____ ____ ____
           6   12   4   20

her gift because of her love and her

____ ____ ____ ____ ____
8   12   14   18   2

in Him.

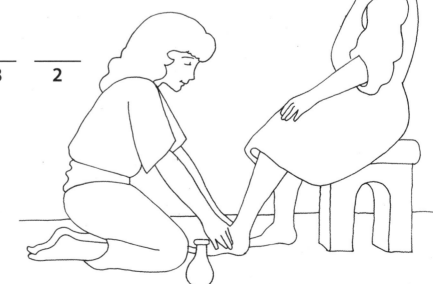

© *Bible* Grade 1

107

1. How can you encourage your friends to grow in their faith? Circle each way that you will encourage others.

I WILL PRAY FOR MY FRIENDS.

I WILL SHARE BIBLE TRUTHS WITH MY FRIENDS.

I WILL PRAY WITH MY FRIENDS.

I WILL REMIND MY FRIENDS THAT GOD LOVES THEM.

I WILL INVITE MY FRIENDS TO GO TO CHURCH WITH ME.

2. Color each shape with a dot to find a hidden word. Write the word on the line to complete the words of Jesus.

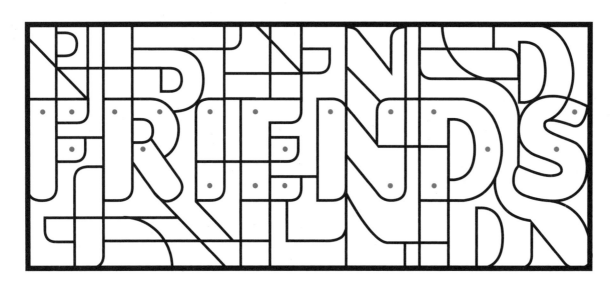

Jesus said, "I have called you _____." John 15:15

The name **Peter** means **a rock**. Peter did not always act like a rock! Big rocks are hard to move, but Peter changed his mind a lot.

Read each of the sentences about Peter and the words on the rocks. Circle the rock that has the words that correctly complete the sentence.

1. Jesus said that Peter and the other disciples would

2. Peter promised Jesus that he would not

3. Jesus said that Peter would

4. That night, Peter lied about knowing Jesus

5. When the rooster crowed, Peter remembered

Jesus forgave Peter. He told Peter, "Feed My sheep." This was Jesus' way of telling Peter that Peter would be a leader in the Church. Peter would lead others to know Jesus. Peter would also teach and care for people who had already accepted Jesus as Savior.

1. Color the sheep that show the only ways for Christians to receive God's forgiveness.

confess sin to God

do good things

pay money

repent

2. What can you do to set a good example for your classmates? Circle the words that show ways that you can be a leader.

OBEY TEACHERS

BE KIND

LISTEN WHEN OTHERS SHARE

HELP IN THE CLASSROOM

CLEAN UP

PRAY FOR CLASSMATES

PLAY WITH EVERYONE

PLAY FAIRLY

Unscramble the letters below each line to make a word that correctly completes each sentence. Write the word.

1. Peter and John met a lame man who begged for _____.

oeymn

2. Peter gave the man something better than _____.

olgd

3. The man praised God that he could _____.

alwk

4. The people wanted to know more about _____.

esJus

5. Peter and John kept on preaching _____.

bdlyol

Complete the chart by writing the words **friends**, **forgave**, **loyal**, **example**, and **confess** on each line to make the sentence true.

1. Omari and Adika were _____.

2. Omari was not _____ to Adika.

3. Omari decided to _____ his sin to Adika.

4. Adika _____ Omari.

5. Omari was a good _____ for the older boys.

Put the words in order to complete each sentence.

1. Jesus showed His power over death when He raised Lazarus

_____.

dead   from   the

2. After Jesus raised Lazarus, He rode a

_____.

donkey   Jerusalem   into

3. The people shouted, "Hosanna! Blessed is He who comes in

_____."

the   Lord   name   of   the

Jesus did everything He did because He loves all people! Read each sentence. Draw a line from the sentence to the correct picture.

1. Jesus washed His disciples' feet. He showed them how to serve one another.

2. Jesus prayed for His disciples.

3. Jesus used bread and wine to help His disciples remember Him.

4. Jesus shared a last meal with His disciples.

Write your name on the blank line. Read the sentences.

5. Jesus prayed for people who would come to know Him, even people who had not yet been born at the time of His prayer (John 17).

Jesus prayed for _____ to come to know and love Him.

Read the sentences. Write the letter of each picture beside the sentences that describe it.

_____ **1.** Jesus was arrested and taken away. When one of the disciples cut off the ear of the high priest's servant, Jesus healed the man.

a.

_____ **2.** Soldiers beat Jesus. They made Jesus wear a crown of thorns and a purple robe. The soldiers made Jesus carry His cross and then nailed Him to it. Jesus let them do this to Him.

b.

c.

_____ **3.** Jesus died on the cross to pay for the sins of all people. He died for them because He loved them.

4. Write one or two sentences telling how you can show your love for others today.

_____

_____

_____

Unscramble the letters to complete the sentences.

1. Mary Magdalene went to the tomb very ___ ___ ___ ___ ___ in the morning. (rylea)

2. The women brought spices and ___ ___ ___ ___ ___ ___ of cloth to finish wrapping Jesus' body. (pstris)

3. When they got to the tomb, the ___ ___ ___ ___ ___ was rolled back. (onste)

4. ___ ___ ___ ___ ___ ___ were there. One asked the women why they were looking for a living person in a tomb. (Aelsng)

5. The angels reminded the women that Jesus had told them He

would rise ___ ___ ___ ___ ___. (aagin)

6. Write the letters from the blue spaces on the lines below.

The angel said, "He is ___ ___ ___ ___ ___!"

1. Underline the words that tell what the disciples did to lead the Church.

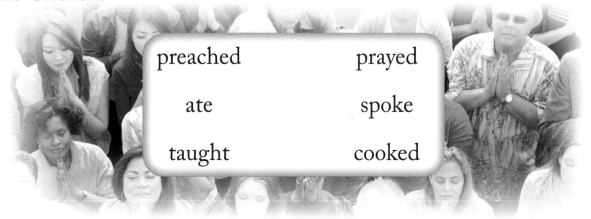

preached   prayed

ate   spoke

taught   cooked

2. Underline the words that tell what the first seven leaders did to lead the Church.

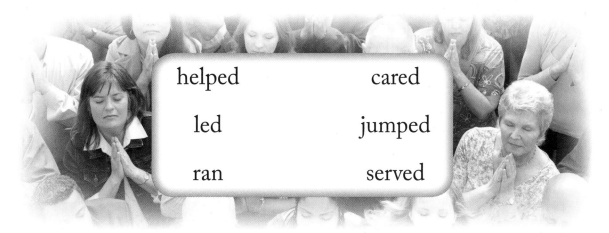

helped   cared

led   jumped

ran   served

3. Underline the words that tell what the people in your church do to lead the Church. Be sure to thank the people who do these things.

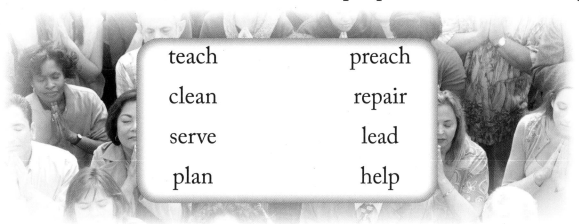

teach   preach

clean   repair

serve   lead

plan   help

Stephen was a servant-leader. First graders can be servant-leaders!

Look at each picture. Write a sentence that tells how the child or children pictured are serving.

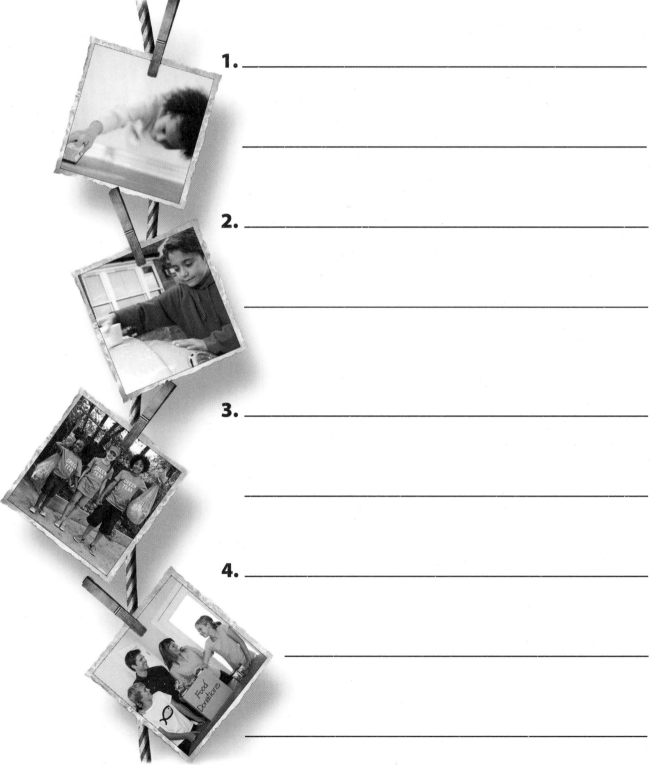

1. _____

_____

2. _____

_____

3. _____

_____

4. _____

_____

Stephen had many qualities of a servant-leader.

1. Circle the things that made Stephen a godly servant-leader.

Stephen had a close relationship with Jesus.

Stephen loved people.

Stephen loved the Lord.

Stephen had courage.

Stephen followed Jesus' teaching.

Stephen showed God's power.

2. Write about how you can be a godly servant-leader.

_____

_____

_____

Read each sentence. Choose the picture of the godly leader that matches the sentence. Write the letter of that picture on the line.

_____ **1.** I showed courage when I faced a giant.

_____ **2.** I showed courage when I led an army of 300 into battle.

_____ **3.** We showed courage when we continued to teach and preach in the name of Jesus.

_____ **4.** I showed courage when I faced the false prophets of Baal.

_____ **5.** I showed courage when I faced the religious leaders and was stoned to death.

A  **B**  **C**  **D**  **E**

Trace the gray words. Read the sentence.

6. Godly leaders serve others willingly, faithfully, and courageously.

Philip shared the good news of Jesus with an Ethiopian man.

Draw a line to match the words with the person who said or might have said them.

I do not understand Isaiah's words. Can you explain them to me?

Do you understand what you are reading?

Who was Isaiah talking about?

Isaiah was talking about the Messiah, Jesus.

Here is some water. Will you baptize me?

Now I understand and believe that Jesus is the Son of God.

Philip obeyed the Lord right away. How should each child obey to follow Philip's example? Fill in the circle.

1. Andy's grandmother comes to pick him up from school. She calls him to come from the playground.
○ Andy should keep playing.
○ Andy should ask why he has to come right away.
○ Andy should run over to his grandmother.

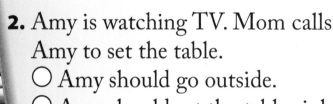

2. Amy is watching TV. Mom calls Amy to set the table.
○ Amy should go outside.
○ Amy should set the table right away.
○ Amy should wait until the TV show is over.

3. Soo Jin wants to play with her friend, but Dad says it is time to go to church.
○ Soo Jin should get in the car.
○ Soo Jin should pretend to be sick.
○ Soo Jin should complain about going to church.

4. Your teacher tells you to put your books away. What should you do?

_____

_____

1. Help Philip find the Ethiopian man. Then help Philip and the man get to the water for baptism. Write words from the maze to correctly complete the sentences.

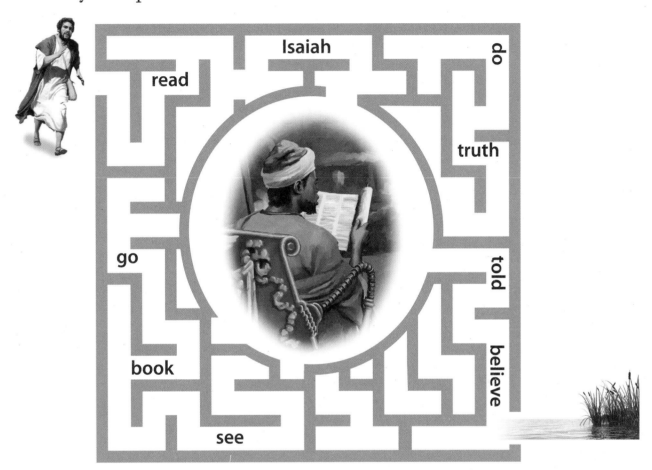

2. The Ethiopian man _____ the book of

_____.

3. Philip _____ the Ethiopian man about Jesus.

4. The man said, "I _____ that Jesus is the Son of God."

Use the Word Bank to write the missing words that complete the invitation to become God's child.

WORD BANK

now	sins	heaven
Jesus	anyone	child

Who may come? _____

What? Become God's _____

When? Right _____

Where? To go to _____

Why? Jesus wants you to be with Him.

He died for your _____!

How? Ask _____ to forgive

you and believe in Him!

1. Jesus spoke to Saul on the road. Saul listened and believed. Color the words that tell about Saul before he came to know the Lord in **black**. Color the words that tell about Saul after he came to know the Lord in **red**.

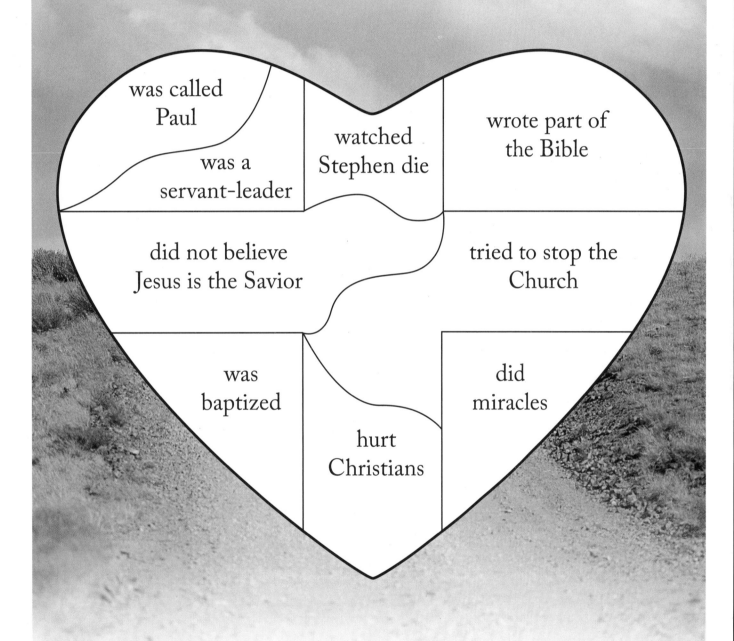

was called
Paul

was a
servant-leader

watched
Stephen die

wrote part of
the Bible

did not believe
Jesus is the Savior

tried to stop the
Church

was
baptized

did
miracles

hurt
Christians

2. Who changed Saul's life and wants to change your life?

_____

Circle every other letter, beginning with **s**, to find a message from God's Word. Write the message on the lines.

Ananias and Paul ____ ____ ____ ____ ____ ____ God

____ ____ ____ ____ ____ ____ ____ ____ ____ ____ ____.

Timothy learned about Jesus and began serving him when he was a young boy. This pleased God!

How can these children please God by their service? Fill in the circle by the best choice.

1. Trevor's mother is a teacher, so Trevor stays after school until his mother finishes her work. Trevor can serve his mother by

   O asking when they can go home.

   O picking up books.

   O leaving a mess in his mother's classroom.

2. Seth needs to be at his game by noon, but his dad has work to do. Seth can serve his dad by

   O helping his dad with the work.

   O watching TV.

   O playing with toys.

3. Ella's parents are greeters at church. Ella can serve her parents and her church by

   O running around outside.

   O passing out church papers.

   O bothering her parents.

Pleasing God

God led many people to help the Church grow. Write the name of the servant or servants to answer each riddle. Their names are **Lydia**, **Aquila** and **Priscilla**, and **Apollos**. One name will be used twice.

1. We are tentmakers. We have a church meeting in our home.

Who are we? _____

2. I sell purple dye and things colored purple.

Who am I? _____

3. I am a Jewish man who knows the Bible very well. I teach others

about Jesus. Who am I? _____

4. I let Paul and his friends stay in my house.

Who am I? _____

5. Unscramble the letters below the banner to complete the sentence.

Faithful service _____ God.

s e l p e a s

Draw a line to match the first part of each sentence to its ending.

1. Paul and Barnabas were •   • Jesus.

2. They went to the synagogue in •   • jealous.

3. Paul told the people about Jesus, the •   • Antioch.

4. Many people believed in •   • missionaries.

5. Some people were •   • stop the missionaries.

6. The jealous people tried to •   • Messiah.

Paul and Barnabas took God's Word to the people of Antioch and Lystra. The people who lived there spoke Greek.

1. Start at the arrow and go down. Circle the letters that are not Greek. Write them in order on the lines.

Paul and Barnabas were ___ ___ ___ ___ ___ ___ ___ ___ of the

___ ___ ___, ___ ___ ___ ___, ___ ___ ___ ___ ___ ___ God!

2. Paul and Barnabas served people out of love for them. Tell how you will lovingly serve others.

_____

_____

Color the hearts that tell ways first graders can serve God.

hearts contain:
- pray for others
- be mean
- help the teacher
- tell others about Jesus
- be unkind to others
- put money in the offering
- listen to the Bible truth
- not share
- show love to one another
- worship God

Use the picture key to name the person that each sentence tells about.

1. explained God's Word to an Ethiopian man.

_____

key

Lottie Moon

Philip

Barnabas

Paul

2. wrote God's Word in the

New Testament.

_____

3. helped Paul take God's Word to

the Gentiles in Lystra.

_____

4. shared God's Word with people in China.

_____

Complete the sentence.

5. I will share God's Word with _____.

1. Use the Word Bank to complete the sentences about Creation.

> **WORD BANK**
>
> people   stars   night   plants   sea

God created day and _____. He spoke and

the sky and the _____ were formed. God

spoke again and dry land appeared. Grass, flowers, trees, and other

_____ grew. God made the sun, moon, and

_____ for the sky. Then God made all kinds

of animals to live in the sea and on the land. Finally, God made

_____.

2. Draw and color the rest of the tree.

God told Adam and Eve not
to eat from the Tree of the
Knowledge of Good and Evil,
but Adam and Eve disobeyed
God and ate some fruit from
that tree. They sinned! They
were sad!

God still loved Adam and
Eve. He loves you, too!

Write the number of each sentence on
the line with the matching picture.

1. Jesus, the Messiah, was born in
a stable in Bethlehem. _____

2. Jesus grew up. He chose 12 men
to be His disciples. _____

3. Jesus was arrested and put on trial.
He was sentenced to die on a cross. _____

4. God raised Jesus from the dead.
He is alive! _____

Make a check mark ✓ on the line by the correct ending.

5. Jesus' death on the cross took the punishment for the sins of _____.

_____ **a.** all people   _____ **b.** all boys   _____ **c.** all girls

6. Because Jesus rose from the dead, Christians will also _____.

_____ **a.** see   _____ **b.** hear   _____ **c.** rise

Trace a path through the maze to the cross. Write a word from the maze to correctly complete each sentence.

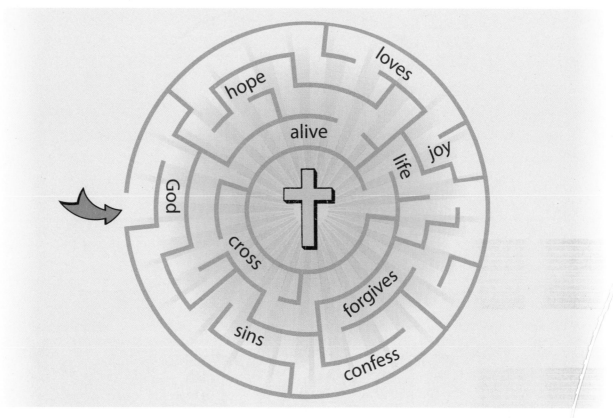

1. Sin separates me from _____.

2. Jesus died to take the punishment for my _____.

3. I _____ my sins to God.

4. Jesus _____ my sins.

5. God gives everlasting _____ to those who believe in Jesus as Savior.

Write words that tell about heaven in each of the ovals.